The Kind Emperor

Stoicism Made Simple: 162 lessons from Marcus Aurelius' Meditations for Kids

B.J. Banks

Smart Coaching Systems Pty Ltd

The Kind Emperor: Stoicism Made Simple: 162 lessons from Marcus Aurelius' Meditations for Kids

© 2024 B.J. Banks
All rights reserved.

No part of this book may be reproduced, distributed, or transmitted in any form or by any means, including photocopying, recording, or other electronic or mechanical methods, without the prior written permission of the publisher, except in the case of brief quotations in reviews and certain noncommercial uses permitted by copyright law.

For permission requests, please contact the publisher at:
Smart Coaching Systems Pty Ltd

www.TheKindEmperor.com

First Edition: November 2024
ISBN: 978-1-7637853-0-4

This book is an interpretation of *Meditations* by Marcus Aurelius, adapted and simplified for a young audience. The ideas presented are inspired by the original work but the ideas are rephrased to be accessible to children, with insights drawn from classical Stoic philosophy.

Contents

Note to Parents	XI
How to Use This Book	
Free Gifts	XIII
Introduction for Children	XIV
1. Mindfulness and Living in the Present	1

   The Gift of a New Day

   Finding Calm Inside

   The Steady Mountain

   Little Moments Matter

   Choose Your Thoughts

   Letting Go of Worries

   Be Here Now

   The Joy of Simply Being

   The Butterfly Moment

   The Sound of Silence

Savoring Each Bite
The Joy of Breathing
Watching the Clouds
The Sandcastle Lesson
Listening with Your Heart
The Adventure of Now
Painting the Moment
The Mirror of Now

2. Wisdom and Learning   21
The Open Book
Everyone Is a Teacher
The Gift of Listening
Learning from Mistakes
The Treasure Hunt
The Wise Owl
Ask and You Shall Learn
The Garden of Knowledge
Patience in Learning
Sharing Your Knowledge
The Mirror of Truth
The Strength of Humility
Learning from Nature
The Power of Books
Wisdom Over Wealth

The Art of Practice
　　　Learning from Challenges
　　　The Company You Keep

3. Kindness and Compassion　　　　　41
　　　The Power of a Smile
　　　Helping Hands
　　　Listening Ears
　　　Sharing Is Caring
　　　The Golden Rule
　　　Forgiving Hearts
　　　Kind Words
　　　Understanding Others
　　　Acts of Kindness
　　　The Ripple Effect
　　　Sharing Happiness
　　　Helping the Earth
　　　Standing Up for Others
　　　The Joy of Giving
　　　Saying "Thank You"
　　　Accepting Differences
　　　Encouraging Others
　　　Being Kind to Yourself

4. Self-Control and Discipline　　　　61
　　　The Power of Patience

Taking Deep Breaths
Taming the Temper
The Discipline of Practice
Choosing Your Actions
The Value of Rules
Overcoming Temptations
Staying Focused
The Quiet Mind
Perseverance Pays Off
Setting Goals
The Reward of Hard Work
Managing Time Wisely
Speaking Kindly
Healthy Habits
Accepting "No" for an Answer
Avoiding Excess
Keeping Promises

5. Courage and Strength 81
   Facing Your Fears
   The Brave Heart
   Standing Up for What's Right
   The Mountain Climber
   Inner Strength
   Facing Challenges with a Smile

    The Hero Inside You
    Admitting Mistakes
    Trying New Things
    The Calm in the Storm
    Believing in Yourself
    Being True to Yourself
    Facing the Unknown
    The Courage to Be Honest
    Overcoming Doubt
    Responding with Kindness
    Courage in Teamwork
    Never Giving Up

6. Honesty and Integrity   101
    The Value of Truth
    Being True to Yourself
    Keeping Promises
    Admitting Mistakes
    The Mirror of Integrity
    Doing the Right Thing
    Standing Firm in Honesty
    Avoiding Gossip
    Honesty in Small Things
    Fair Play
    Respecting Others' Property

  Avoiding Excuses
  The Weight of Lies
  Honesty Builds Trust
  The Ripple Effect of Integrity
  Honesty in Thoughts and Words
  The Joy of a Clear Conscience
  Integrity Lasts a Lifetime

7. Acceptance and Dealing with Change   121
  Embracing Change
  The River of Life
  Letting Go
  Growing Up
  The Caterpillar to Butterfly
  The Weather Within
  Finding the Silver Lining
  The Unchanging Core
  Flexibility is Strength
  Learning from Change
  Accepting Mistakes
  Change is Natural
  Moving Forward
  Accepting Help
  The Puzzle of Life
  Accepting What We Cannot Change

    Growing Through Challenges
    The Adventure of Life

8. Gratitude and Appreciation   141
    A Thankful Heart
    Appreciating Simple Joys
    Gratitude Journal
    Cherishing Friendships
    Thanking Nature
    The Gift of Learning
    Gratitude in Challenges
    Sharing Appreciation
    Grateful for Yourself
    The Magic of Giving
    Thankful for Differences
    Gratitude for Challenges
    Appreciating Effort
    Thanking Your Body
    The Gift of Imagination
    Gratitude for Rest
    Appreciating Kindness
    Gratitude Every Day

9. Patience and Perseverance   161
    The Slow and Steady Turtle
    The Growing Seed

Practice Makes Perfect
Overcoming Obstacles
The Art of Patience
Small Steps Forward
Handling Frustration
The Waiting Game
Patience with Others
Never Giving Up
The Puzzle Piece
The Calm Mind
The Value of Persistence
Patience with Yourself
The Storybook Journey
Waiting Your Turn
The Mountain Stream
Celebrating Small Victories

Afterword	180
Free Gifts	182

Note to Parents

Dear Parents and Caregivers,

Welcome to **The Kind Emperor**, a special adaptation of Marcus Aurelius's **Meditations** for young readers. Marcus Aurelius, a Roman emperor and Stoic philosopher, wrote about ethics, personal growth, and the human experience. Though written almost 2,000 years ago, his ideas still inspire today.

This book introduces children to his wisdom in simple, relevant, and engaging language. Each chapter covers themes like kindness, courage, and mindfulness, making the lessons accessible for children around age eight. My hope is to spark meaningful conversations between you and your child while teaching valuable life skills.

How to Use This Book

- **Daily Reading:** Read one passage a day with your child for reflection.

- **Open Dialogue:** Use these lessons as conversation starters about their everyday experiences and how they might relate to something in their life.

- **Personal Connection:** Share your own experiences related to the themes for deeper understanding, and to strengthen your bond with your child.

In a changing world, virtues like empathy, resilience, and kindness are more important than ever. We hope this book becomes a meaningful part of your family's journey toward growth and connection.

Warm regards,

B.J. Banks

Free Gifts

As a thank you for purchasing The Kind Emperor, I have created 3 practical games and activities to further promote a stoic mindset at home.

Introduction for Children

Hello, young reader!

A long time ago, in a place called Rome, there lived a wise and kind emperor named Marcus Aurelius.

An emperor is like a king, and Marcus was known for being fair and thoughtful. He loved to think about big ideas and write down his thoughts about how to be happy, kind, and brave.

Marcus wrote these ideas in a special book called "Meditations." Even though he lived almost 2,000 years ago, his words are still important today!

This book is a collection of Marcus's ideas, rewritten just for you.

Each page shares a simple lesson to help you learn about yourself and the world around you. You'll find lessons about being a good friend, staying calm when things are hard, and enjoying every moment.

Are you ready to discover the wisdom of Marcus Aurelius?

Let's dive in and explore these timeless lessons together!

CHAPTER I

Mindfulness and Living in the Present

LEARN HOW TO ENJOY EACH MOMENT BY FOCUSING ON THE "NOW" AND APPRECIATING THE WORLD AROUND YOU.

The Gift of a New Day

Marcus Aurelius teaches us to appreciate each new day as a fresh opportunity to embrace life's simple joys.

When you wake up each morning, think about how special it is to be alive.

Feel the warm sun, hear the birds sing, and know that today is a new adventure.

Be happy for the chance to learn, play, and love others.

What is something you are grateful for today?

Finding Calm Inside

Marcus suggests that inner peace can be found by retreating into our minds, no matter the chaos around us.

Imagine you have a quiet place inside your mind, like a secret garden or a cozy fort.

When things get loud or busy, you can close your eyes and visit this calm place.

It's always there to help you feel peaceful and safe.

Let's create your own calm place. What would it look like?

The Steady Mountain

He compares a resilient mind to a solid mountain that remains unmoved by life's challenges.

Think of yourself as a tall mountain.

The wind blows, and storms may come, but you stay strong and steady.

When you feel upset, remember you're like that mountain.

Strong and unshakable inside.

When was a time you stayed strong like a mountain?

Little Moments Matter

Marcus encourages us to find meaning and joy in the small, everyday moments.

Every moment is special, like a tiny treasure.

When you draw a picture, enjoy each color you use.

When you read a book, get lost in the story.

By paying attention to little moments, you can find joy all around you.

What little moment today made you smile?

Choose Your Thoughts

He emphasizes that while we can't control events, we can choose how we think about them.

You can't always choose what happens, but you can choose how you think about it.

If plans change, you can feel grumpy or you can look for something fun to do instead.

Picking happy thoughts can make your day brighter!

How can you change a grumpy thought into a happy one?

Letting Go of Worries

He advises letting go of unnecessary worries that distract us from enjoying the present.

Sometimes, worries can feel like heavy backpacks.

Imagine taking off that backpack and setting it down.

Without the extra weight, you can run, play, and have more fun.

Let go of worries, and enjoy your day!

What's a worry you have right now that you could let go of?

Be Here Now

Marcus teaches us to fully engage with whatever we are doing in the present.

Whatever you're doing, be there completely.

If you're building with blocks, focus on your tower.

If you're singing a song, sing with all your heart.

Being fully present makes everything more enjoyable!

How can you focus on what you're doing right now?

The Joy of Simply Being

He encourages finding happiness in the simplicity of being alive, without needing more.

You don't need anything fancy to be happy.

Just being yourself is wonderful!

Feel the breeze on your face, wiggle your toes, and know that being you is something to celebrate every day.

What do you love about being you?

The Butterfly Moment

Marcus reminds us to appreciate fleeting moments that may never come again.

Imagine a beautiful butterfly landing on your hand.

It might stay for just a moment before flying away.

If you're paying attention, you'll get to see its colorful wings up close.

But if you're distracted, you might miss it.

Try to notice the special little things that happen around you every day!

What small, special thing can you notice right now?

The Sound of Silence

He highlights the value of finding peace in moments of quiet and stillness.

Sometimes, it's nice to sit quietly and listen.

You might hear birds chirping, leaves rustling, or your own heartbeat.

Taking a moment to enjoy the quiet can make you feel calm and happy inside.

What sounds do you hear when you sit quietly?

Savoring Each Bite

Marcus encourages mindfulness, even in small actions like eating, to deepen our appreciation of life.

When you eat your favorite food, take small bites and really taste it.

Notice the flavors and textures.

Eating slowly not only helps you enjoy your meal more but also makes your tummy feel happier!

Go eat something yummy. Eat it slowly, and really taste it.

The Joy of Breathing

He suggests that focusing on our breath can help us stay present and calm.

Take a deep breath in, and then let it out slowly.

Feel the air fill your lungs and then leave again.

Focusing on your breathing can help you feel calm and connected to the world around you.

Stop and take a big deep breath. How do you feel?

Watching the Clouds

Marcus teaches us that observing nature is a way to stay grounded in the present.

Lie down on the grass and look up at the sky.

Watch the clouds as they change shapes.

Maybe you'll see a dragon, a ship, or a funny face!

Enjoying the clouds helps you relax and appreciate the moment.

Have you ever seen any shapes in the clouds?

The Sandcastle Lesson

He reminds us that moments are temporary, but the joy in experiencing them remains valuable.

When you build a sandcastle at the beach, you know the waves might wash it away.

But building it is still lots of fun!

Enjoy making your castle without worrying about how long it will last.

The fun is in the doing!

What's something fun you enjoyed today, even if it didn't last long?

Listening with Your Heart

Marcus emphasizes the importance of fully listening to others to connect more deeply.

When a friend is talking to you, listen carefully to their words.

Look at their face and try to understand how they feel.

Listening with your heart shows you care and helps you be a better friend.

How can you show someone you're really listening to them?

The Adventure of Now

He encourages us to approach each day with curiosity, seeing every moment as an adventure.

Treat every day like it's a new quest!

What exciting things will you discover today?

Maybe you'll learn a new game, find a cool rock, or meet someone new.

Embrace each moment as part of your grand adventure!

What new adventure or discovery will you find today?

Painting the Moment

Marcus teaches that expressing the present through creativity helps us appreciate it more.

Draw or paint what you see around you right now.

Maybe it's your pet, a tree outside, or your favorite toy.

Creating art about the present helps you see and appreciate what's in front of you.

What would you draw or paint from what you see right now?

The Mirror of Now

He encourages self-reflection to better understand ourselves in the present moment.

Look in the mirror and smile at yourself.

Think about how you feel right now.

Happy? Excited? Thoughtful?

Recognizing your feelings helps you understand yourself better and enjoy the moment.

How do you feel right now, and what makes you feel that way?

CHAPTER 2

Wisdom and Learning

DISCOVER THE JOY OF LEARNING NEW THINGS AND HOW GAINING WISDOM HELPS YOU GROW EVERY DAY.

The Open Book

Marcus Aurelius emphasizes the importance of being open to learning throughout life.

Your mind is like a book with empty pages, ready to be filled with stories and knowledge.

Every day, you can learn something new, like how plants grow, why the sky is blue, or how to tie your shoes.

Be curious, ask questions, and enjoy filling your book!

What new thing did you learn today that you can add to your book?

Everyone Is a Teacher

He suggests that we can learn something valuable from every person we meet.

Every person you meet knows something you don't.

Your friends, family, teachers, and even new people can teach you amazing things.

Listen closely, and you might discover a new game, a funny joke, or a cool fact about the world!

What is something new you've learned from a friend or family member?

The Gift of Listening

Marcus highlights the wisdom gained from listening more than speaking.

You have two ears and one mouth so you can listen twice as much as you talk!

When you listen carefully, you learn lots of interesting things and show others that you care about what they have to say.

When was a time you listened carefully and learned something surprising?

Learning from Mistakes

He views mistakes as opportunities for growth and gaining wisdom.

It's okay to make mistakes, that's how we learn!

If you spill your milk, you'll learn to be more careful next time.

Each mistake is like a stepping stone that helps you get better and smarter.

What's a mistake you made recently that you could learn something from?

The Treasure Hunt

Seeking knowledge is like searching for hidden treasure.

Imagine that learning new things is like going on a treasure hunt.

Every fact you discover or skill you learn is a shiny gem or a gold coin.

The more you explore, the richer your mind becomes!

Where do you think you could find some more treasure from?

The Wise Owl

Wisdom comes from observing and reflecting on experiences.

Be like a wise owl who watches and thinks.

When you see something happen, take a moment to think about it.

Why did it happen?

What can you learn from it?

This helps you understand the world better!

How could you be more like the wise owl?

Ask and You Shall Learn

Encouraging curiosity and the asking of questions.

Never be afraid to ask "Why?" or "How?"

Questions are like keys that unlock the secrets of the world.

The more you ask, the more you know!

What question do you have right now that could help you learn something new? Ask it!

The Garden of Knowledge

Cultivating the mind is like tending to a garden.

Think of your mind as a garden.

Learning new things is like planting seeds.

The more you learn, the more your garden grows.

Blooming with colorful flowers of ideas and thoughts!

What new "seed" of knowledge can you plant in your mind today?

Patience in Learning

Understanding that gaining wisdom takes time and effort.

Learning something new can take time, just like a tree takes time to grow.

Be patient and keep trying, and soon you'll see how much you've grown!

What is something you are practicing now that you want to get better at?

Sharing Your Knowledge

Wisdom is not just for oneself but to be shared with others.

When you learn something cool, share it with your friends!

Teaching others helps you understand it better and spreads the joy of learning.

What can you teach a friend that you've learned recently?

The Mirror of Truth

Self-reflection is essential for personal growth and wisdom.

Take time to think about your day.

What did you do well?

What could you do differently next time?

Looking into your own "mirror" helps you learn more about yourself!

What did you learn about yourself today?

The Strength of Humility

Recognizing that there's always more to learn keeps us humble.

No matter how much you know, there's always more to discover!

Stay humble and excited about learning new things every day.

What is something you'd like to learn more about?

Learning from Nature

Nature teaches us valuable lessons if we pay attention.

Watch how birds build nests or how plants grow toward the sun.

Nature is a great teacher, showing us amazing things about patience, hard work, and beauty!

Have you ever watched something in nature?

The Power of Books

Books are a source of wisdom and knowledge from others.

Books are like magic portals to different worlds and ideas.

When you read, you can go on adventures, learn new things, and meet interesting characters.

Dive into a book and see where it takes you!

What book took you on a great adventure?

Wisdom Over Wealth

Valuing wisdom more than material possessions.

Having lots of toys is fun, but knowing lots of things is even better!

Wisdom stays with you forever and helps you make good choices.

What's something you know that is really interesting?

The Art of Practice

Skills improve with practice and dedication.

Want to get better at drawing, playing an instrument, or a sport?

Practice is the secret!

The more you do something, the better you become.

Keep at it, and you'll see amazing progress!

If you could be better at something in 4 weeks time, what would it be?

You can start practicing today!

Learning from Challenges

Difficulties can teach us important lessons.

When something is hard, don't give up!

Challenges help you grow stronger and smarter.

Every time you overcome one, you learn and become more confident.

What is a challenge you are trying to overcome at the moment?

The Company You Keep

Surrounding oneself with good influences fosters wisdom.

Spend time with friends who make good choices and encourage you to do the same.

Good friends help each other learn and grow!

Who are the friends that help you make good choices and learn new things?

Do you know anyone else who you think might be a good friend?

CHAPTER 3

Kindness and Compassion

FIND OUT HOW BEING KIND AND UNDERSTANDING TOWARD OTHERS MAKES THE WORLD A HAPPIER PLACE.

The Power of a Smile

Marcus Aurelius emphasizes treating others with kindness and understanding.

Your smile is like a bright sun that can make someone's day better.

When you smile at a friend or even someone you don't know well, you spread happiness.

Try sharing your smile today!

Who can you share a smile with today to brighten their day?

Helping Hands

He encourages helping others as part of our duty to humanity.

If you see someone who needs help, like reaching a high shelf or carrying something heavy, offer your helping hands.

Little acts of kindness make the world a friendlier place!

What are some ways you could help others?

Listening Ears

Being a good listener shows compassion and respect.

When a friend is talking, listen carefully.

Sometimes, they might just need someone to hear them.

Using your listening ears shows you care about how they feel.

What are some things you can do to be a good listener to a friend?

Sharing Is Caring

He highlights the importance of sharing what we have with others.

If you have extra snacks or toys, think about sharing them with others.

Sharing not only makes others happy but also fills your heart with joy!

When was the last time you shared something with someone, without being asked?

The Golden Rule

Treat others as you would like to be treated.

Think about how you like to be treated.

With kindness, respect, and friendliness.

Try to treat others the same way, and you'll make many friends!

How can you treat others the way you want to be treated?

Forgiving Hearts

Forgiveness is a key aspect of compassion.

If someone says they're sorry for hurting your feelings, try to forgive them.

Holding onto anger is like carrying a heavy backpack.

Let it go, and you'll feel lighter and happier!

Who can you forgive today to feel lighter inside?

Kind Words

Words have the power to uplift or hurt; choose them wisely.

Your words are powerful.

Saying kind things like "Great job!" or "Thank you!" can make someone's day.

Think before you speak, and choose words that spread kindness.

What kind words can you say to someone to make them feel good?

Understanding Others

Empathy helps us connect and be compassionate.

Try to imagine how others feel.

If a friend is sad because they lost a game, offer a hug or encouraging words.

Understanding feelings helps you be a better friend.

What are some signs that one of your friends might be sad?

Acts of Kindness

Small acts can have a big impact on others.

Doing little things, like holding the door open or picking up trash, makes the world nicer.

Every act of kindness counts!

What small act of kindness can you do today?

The Ripple Effect

Kindness spreads from one person to another.

When you're kind to someone, they might be kind to another person, like a chain reaction.

Your kindness can start a wave of good feelings that spreads far and wide!

How could you start a wave of kindness?

Sharing Happiness

Rejoicing in others' happiness shows a generous spirit.

When something good happens to a friend, like winning a game or getting a new pet, be happy for them!

Sharing in their joy makes your friendship stronger.

How can you show happiness for someone else's success?

Helping the Earth

Compassion extends to caring for our environment.

Being kind isn't just for people, it's for animals and nature, too!

Plant a tree, feed the birds, or recycle.

Taking care of the Earth shows compassion for all living things.

What can you do today to show kindness to the Earth?

Standing Up for Others

Protecting those who are vulnerable is a compassionate act.

If you see someone being teased or left out, invite them to join your game or tell an adult.

Standing up for others shows bravery and kindness.

How can you stand up for someone who needs help?

The Joy of Giving

Giving without expecting anything in return brings inner happiness.

Making a card for someone or giving a small gift just because can make both of you feel happy inside.

Giving is its own special reward!

Who is someone you would like to make someone feel special?

Saying "Thank You"

Expressing gratitude is a form of kindness.

When someone does something nice for you, like helping with homework or cooking your favorite meal, say "Thank you!"

It shows you appreciate them and makes them feel good.

Who can you say "Thank you" to today to show your appreciation?

Accepting Differences

Respecting and embracing diversity is compassionate.

People are like colorful crayons.

Each one is different and special.

Accepting and celebrating these differences makes the world more beautiful!

What is something special about a friend that makes them different and unique?

Encouraging Others

Supporting others in their efforts shows kindness.

If a friend is nervous about a test or performance, tell them "You can do it!"

Your encouragement can boost their confidence and help them succeed.

Who can you encourage to help them feel more confident?

Being Kind to Yourself

Self-compassion is important for overall kindness.

Don't forget to be kind to yourself!

If you make a mistake, forgive yourself and try again.

Taking care of yourself helps you be happier and kinder to others.

What's something you could be kinder to yourself about?

CHAPTER 4

Self-Control and Discipline

EXPLORE WAYS TO MANAGE YOUR ACTIONS AND EMOTIONS TO MAKE GOOD CHOICES AND FEEL PROUD OF YOURSELF.

The Power of Patience

Marcus Aurelius emphasizes the importance of patience and controlling one's impulses.

Sometimes you might want something right now, like a snack before dinner or a new toy.

But waiting patiently is important.

Patience is like a superpower that helps you make good choices and feel proud of yourself!

What is something you find hard to wait for sometimes?

Taking Deep Breaths

He suggests that taking a moment to pause can help control emotions.

When you feel angry or upset, stop and take a few deep breaths.

Imagine blowing out candles on a birthday cake.

This can help you feel calmer and think more clearly.

Can you think of a time where it would have been good to take some deep breaths?

Taming the Temper

Managing anger and not letting it control you.

Anger can feel like a wild horse inside you.

But you can be the rider who gently calms the horse.

By staying in control, you can choose to speak kindly and solve problems peacefully.

How can you calm your "wild horse" when you feel angry?

The Discipline of Practice

Discipline is key to mastering any skill.

Want to get better at piano, soccer, or drawing?

Practice regularly, even when it's hard.

Discipline is like watering a plant, it helps your talents grow!

What skill will you practice today to help it grow?

Choosing Your Actions

We have control over our actions, even if we can't control everything else.

You can't control the weather or what others do, but you can control what you do.

Choose actions that are kind and helpful, and you'll feel good inside.

What kind action will you choose to do today?

The Value of Rules

Understanding that rules help us and require discipline to follow.

Rules, like bedtime or taking turns, are there to keep you safe and fair.

Following rules shows you have self-control and respect for others.

What rule do you find hard to follow?

Overcoming Temptations

Resisting temptations leads to strength of character.

If you really want an extra cookie but know it's not allowed, saying "No thank you" makes you strong.

Every time you resist a temptation, you become better at making good choices.

What temptation will you resist today to practice self-control?

Staying Focused

Concentration is important for achieving goals.

When you're doing homework or a project, try to focus without getting distracted.

Staying focused helps you finish tasks faster and better!

What can you focus on today to finish it faster?

The Quiet Mind

Inner peace comes from controlling one's thoughts.

Your mind can be like a calm pond or a stormy sea.

By thinking peaceful thoughts and letting go of worries, you can keep your mind quiet and happy.

What peaceful thoughts make you feel calm and happy?

Perseverance Pays Off

Sticking with tasks even when they are challenging.

If a puzzle is hard, don't give up!

Keep trying, and you'll feel amazing when you finish it.

Perseverance means not quitting when things are tough.

What challenge will you keep trying at today to succeed?

Setting Goals

Having clear goals helps maintain discipline.

Decide what you want to achieve, like reading a whole book or learning to swim.

Setting goals gives you something to work toward and helps you stay on track.

What is a goal you would love to achieve?

The Reward of Hard Work

Hard work leads to satisfaction and success.

When you work hard at something, like cleaning your room or practicing a skill, you'll feel proud of what you've accomplished.

Hard work brings happiness!

What can you work hard at today to feel proud of yourself?

Managing Time Wisely

Time management is a form of self-discipline.

Plan your time so you can do your homework, play, and rest.

Managing your time helps you enjoy all the things you like to do without rushing.

How could you manage your time to enjoy both work and play?

Speaking Kindly

Controlling our words to avoid hurting others.

Think before you speak.

If your words might hurt someone's feelings, choose kinder ones instead.

Using kind words shows you have control over what you say.

Instead of getting mad, what's something kind you can say instead next time?

Healthy Habits

Discipline in taking care of one's body.

Brushing your teeth, eating fruits and veggies, and getting enough sleep are healthy habits.

Taking care of your body helps you feel good and have energy to play!

Do you have any healthy habits?

Accepting "No" for an Answer

Understanding and accepting limits set by others.

Sometimes parents or teachers might say "No" to something you want.

Accepting their answer calmly shows maturity and self-control.

How will you handle hearing "No" today with maturity?

Avoiding Excess

Not overindulging in pleasures.

It's fun to watch TV or play video games, but too much isn't good.

Balance your fun activities with other things like reading, playing outside, or helping at home.

Is there something that you often do for too long or too much?

Keeping Promises

Being reliable by doing what you say you will do.

If you promise to help with dishes or meet a friend to play, make sure you do it.

Keeping promises shows you are responsible and trustworthy.

What promise will you keep today to show responsibility?

CHAPTER 5

Courage and Strength

LEARN HOW TO BE BRAVE AND STRONG, EVEN WHEN THINGS FEEL SCARY OR DIFFICULT.

Facing Your Fears

Marcus Aurelius emphasizes the importance of confronting fears and not letting them control you.

Everyone feels scared sometimes, and that's okay.

Maybe you're afraid of the dark or trying something new.

Being brave means trying your best even when you feel scared.

When you face your fears, you become stronger!

What is one fear you can face today to help you grow stronger?

The Brave Heart

He suggests that true courage comes from within and is a matter of character.

Being brave isn't about not feeling afraid, it's about doing the right thing even when you are.

Your heart is strong, and it helps you be courageous in tough times.

Remember, bravery comes from inside you!

What brave action can you take today, even if you feel a little scared?

Standing Up for What's Right

He encourages standing up for justice and doing what's right, even when it's difficult.

If you see someone being unkind, it's important to speak up or tell a grown-up.

Standing up for others shows courage and helps make the world a better place.

Have you ever stood up for someone before?

The Mountain Climber

Overcoming obstacles builds strength and character.

Imagine climbing a big mountain.

It might be hard and tiring, but each step you take makes you stronger.

Overcoming challenges helps you grow and shows how strong you really are!

What big challenge can you take one forward on today?

Inner Strength

True strength comes from within, not just physical abilities.

You might not be the biggest or strongest, but your inner strength, like kindness, honesty, and bravery, is what truly matters.

This strength inside helps you handle anything!

What is your biggest inner strength?

Facing Challenges with a Smile

Approaching difficulties with a positive attitude demonstrates courage.

When something is hard, like a tricky puzzle, try tackling it with a smile.

Believing in yourself and staying positive makes challenges easier to overcome.

What challenge can you face today with a smile?

The Hero Inside You

Everyone has the potential to be a hero through their actions.

You don't need a cape to be a hero.

Helping others, telling the truth, and being brave makes you a real-life hero!

How can you be a hero to someone today?

Admitting Mistakes

Having the courage to admit when you're wrong.

If you make a mistake, like breaking something or hurting someone's feelings, it takes courage to say "I'm sorry."

Admitting mistakes helps you learn and shows you're strong inside.

What mistake can you admit to today to show your inner strength?

Trying New Things

Stepping out of your comfort zone is an act of bravery.

Trying a new food, game, or activity can be scary but also exciting!

Being open to new experiences helps you grow and discover what you love.

What new thing will you try today to step out of your comfort zone?

The Calm in the Storm

Maintaining composure in stressful situations is a sign of strength.

When things get hectic, like during a big game or a busy day, staying calm helps you think clearly.

Being the "calm in the storm" shows inner strength and helps others feel calm too.

How can you stay calm today when things get busy?

Believing in Yourself

Self-confidence is a key aspect of courage.

Believe that you can do it!

Whether it's reading aloud in class or making a new friend, trusting yourself gives you the courage to try.

Can you think of a time when you believed in yourself?

Being True to Yourself

It takes courage to be true to oneself and not just follow the crowd.

It's okay to be different!

Wearing your favorite clothes or liking unique hobbies makes you special.

Being yourself is a brave and wonderful thing.

How can you be true to yourself today and celebrate what makes you unique?

Facing the Unknown

Embracing uncertainty with courage.

New places or experiences can feel strange or scary, like starting a new school.

Remember that every adventure begins with a first step.

Facing the unknown helps you discover exciting things!

What unknown will you face today to start a new adventure?

The Courage to Be Honest

Telling the truth, even when it's hard, is a courageous act.

If you broke a rule or made a mistake, telling the truth might be tough.

But being honest shows you're brave and trustworthy.

What truth will you tell today to show your courage?

Overcoming Doubt

Not letting self-doubt prevent you from taking action.

Sometimes you might think, "I can't do this."

But trying anyway helps you see how strong you really are.

Don't let doubt stop you from doing your best!

What can you try today that you may have been scared of before?

Responding with Kindness

Responding to unkindness with kindness requires courage.

If someone is mean to you, responding with kindness can be hard but powerful.

Your kindness might even help them become nicer!

How can you respond with kindness, even if someone is unkind?

Courage in Teamwork

Working together and relying on others is a form of strength.

Being part of a team means helping each other.

It takes courage to trust your teammates and work together to achieve a goal.

Have you ever achieved anything as part of a team?

Never Giving Up

Perseverance in the face of ongoing challenges shows great courage.

Even when things are really tough, like a long hike or a big project, keep going!

Never giving up shows that you're brave and strong inside.

What challenge will you keep going on today to show your inner strength?

CHAPTER 6

Honesty and Integrity

UNDERSTAND THE IMPORTANCE OF TELLING THE TRUTH AND BEING TRUE TO YOURSELF AND OTHERS.

The Value of Truth

Marcus Aurelius emphasizes the importance of speaking the truth and being honest in all dealings.

Always tell the truth, even when it's hard.

Telling the truth builds trust, and people will know they can count on you.

Honesty is like a shining light that guides you and others in the right direction.

Can you remember a moment where it was hard to tell the truth?

Being True to Yourself

He encourages individuals to live authentically and stay true to their values.

Be yourself!

Don't pretend to be someone you're not just to impress others.

Your true self is wonderful, and being honest about who you are makes you special and unique.

How can you be true to yourself today and show others the real you?

Keeping Promises

Keeping one's word is a key aspect of integrity.

If you promise to help your friend or finish a chore, make sure you do it.

Keeping your promises shows that you are reliable and can be trusted.

What is a promise you have kept?

Admitting Mistakes

He believes in acknowledging errors openly and learning from them.

If you make a mistake, like spilling juice or breaking something, tell the truth about it.

Admitting mistakes helps you fix them and shows you are honest and brave.

What mistake can you admit to today to show your honesty?

The Mirror of Integrity

Living with integrity allows one to have a clear conscience.

Imagine looking in a mirror and feeling proud of who you see.

When you're honest and do the right thing, you can feel good about yourself and have a happy heart.

What is something you have done that makes you feel proud?

Doing the Right Thing

Marcus emphasizes acting rightly even when no one is watching.

Doing the right thing isn't just for when others are watching.

Even if you're alone, making good choices shows you're a person of integrity.

Have you ever done the right thing when no one was watching?

Standing Firm in Honesty

He encourages standing by the truth, even if it's difficult.

Sometimes telling the truth might seem hard, especially if you're worried about getting in trouble.

But being honest is always the best choice and helps you grow stronger inside.

Have you ever been scared of getting in trouble and decided not to tell the truth?

Avoiding Gossip

Refraining from speaking ill of others is part of living with integrity.

Talking badly about others can hurt feelings and spread unkindness.

Instead, speak kindly or not at all.

This shows respect and honesty toward others.

What is something nice you can say about someone you don't like?

Honesty in Small Things

Integrity is shown in small actions as well as big ones.

Even little things, like not taking something that isn't yours or telling the truth about finishing your homework, matter.

Being honest in small ways builds your character.

What small honest action can you take today to build your character?

Fair Play

Playing fair and following the rules is a form of honesty.

When playing games, follow the rules and be fair.

Cheating might seem tempting, but winning honestly feels much better and keeps the game fun for everyone.

Have you ever overcome the temptation to cheat at a game? Was it hard?

Respecting Others' Property

Honesty involves respecting what belongs to others.

If something isn't yours, like a toy or a pencil, ask before using it.

Taking care of others' things shows respect and honesty.

How can you show respect for others' belongings today?

Avoiding Excuses

He advises against making excuses to avoid responsibility.

If you forget to do something, like clean your room, don't make excuses.

Accepting responsibility shows honesty and helps you remember next time.

How can you take responsibility for something today without making excuses?

The Weight of Lies

Lies can burden the soul, while truth brings freedom.

Telling lies can feel like carrying a heavy backpack all the time.

Telling the truth lightens your load and makes you feel free and happy.

Have you ever told a lie that has caused you to feel bad afterwards? What could you do to fix it?

Honesty Builds Trust

Trust is built through consistent honesty.

When you're honest, people know they can count on you.

Trust is like a strong bridge between you and others, built by being truthful every day.

What are some ways you could build more trust with the people around you?

The Ripple Effect of Integrity

Your integrity can inspire others to act honestly.

When you choose to be honest, you encourage others to do the same.

Your good example can spread honesty and kindness all around!

How can you set an example of honesty today for others to follow?

Honesty in Thoughts and Words

Integrity involves aligning thoughts and words with actions.

Think good thoughts, speak truthful words, and do the right things.

When all parts of you work together honestly, you feel whole and happy.

What honest thought, word, and action will you choose today?

The Joy of a Clear Conscience

Living honestly brings inner peace and joy.

When you're honest, you don't have to worry or feel guilty.

A clear conscience is like a sunny day inside you, bringing joy and peace.

What can you do today to keep your conscience clear and feel joyful inside?

Integrity Lasts a Lifetime

Integrity is a lifelong commitment that shapes who you are.

Being honest and true to yourself isn't just for today, it's something you can carry with you always.

Integrity is a treasure that lasts a lifetime!

How will you practice integrity today so it stays with you forever?

CHAPTER 7

Acceptance and Dealing with Change

DISCOVER HOW ACCEPTING CHANGES CAN LEAD TO NEW ADVENTURES AND HELP YOU GROW.

Embracing Change

Marcus Aurelius teaches that change is a natural part of life and accepting it leads to peace.

Just like the seasons change from spring to summer to fall and winter, things in our lives change too.

You might move to a new house, get a new teacher, or make new friends.

Embracing change can bring new adventures and help you grow!

What is one change in your life that has lead to a new adventure?

# The River of Life

He compares life to a flowing river, always moving and changing.

Imagine life is like a river, always flowing and never stopping.

The water you see today isn't the same as yesterday.

Enjoy the ride and see where the river takes you!

How can you enjoy the ride of life's changes today?

Letting Go

Accepting that we cannot control everything and letting go of what we cannot change.

Sometimes things happen that we can't control, like a canceled trip or a rainy day.

Instead of feeling upset, try to let go and find something fun to do instead.

Letting go can make you feel lighter and happier!

What can you let go of today to feel happier inside?

Growing Up

Understanding that growing and changing is a natural part of life.

You're not the same person you were a year ago.

You've grown taller, learned new things, and maybe your favorite color has changed.

Growing up is exciting, and each new stage brings new things to discover!

What exciting new thing have you discovered as you've grown?

The Caterpillar to Butterfly

Change can lead to beautiful transformations.

Think about how a caterpillar turns into a butterfly.

At first, it might seem scary to change, but it becomes something amazing!

Just like the butterfly, changes in your life can lead to wonderful new things.

What change in your life could lead to something amazing?

The Weather Within

Just as we accept changes in the weather, we can accept changes in our feelings.

Some days you might feel sunny and happy, other days cloudy or sad.

It's okay to have different feelings, they change just like the weather.

Accepting your feelings helps you understand yourself better.

Can you remember a time when you were sad, but it didn't last forever?

Finding the Silver Lining

Looking for the good in every situation, even when things change unexpectedly.

If plans change or something doesn't go your way, try to find the good in it.

Maybe the picnic got rained out, but now you can have a fun indoor picnic!

Looking for the bright side makes changes easier to handle.

Have you ever found the silver lining in a bad situation?

The Unchanging Core

While everything changes, your inner self remains constant.

Even though lots of things change around you, like where you live or what school you go to, you're still you inside!

Your kindness, your smile, and your favorite jokes stay with you wherever you go.

What part of you stays the same no matter what changes around you?

Flexibility is Strength

Being flexible and adaptable is a strength that helps us deal with change.

Think of yourself like a tree that bends in the wind.

By being flexible, you won't break when things change.

Being able to adjust helps you stay strong and happy!

How can you be flexible today when something changes?

Learning from Change

Each change brings an opportunity to learn something new.

When something changes, like starting a new class, it's a chance to learn new things and meet new friends.

Change can be like opening a door to new adventures!

What can you learn from a change happening in your life right now?

Accepting Mistakes

Accepting mistakes as part of learning and growing.

Everyone makes mistakes, and that's okay!

Accepting them helps you learn and do better next time.

Mistakes are like stepping stones on the path to success.

What mistake can you accept today as a chance to learn and grow?

Change is Natural

Recognizing that change is a natural part of the universe.

Just as the moon changes shape each night and flowers bloom and fade, change is a natural part of life.

Understanding this can help you feel more comfortable when things change.

What change can you feel more comfortable with, knowing it's natural?

Moving Forward

Focusing on the present and future rather than clinging to the past.

Instead of holding onto what was, look forward to what's coming next!

Each new day is a chance for new fun and experiences.

Moving forward helps you grow and find happiness.

What exciting thing are you looking forward to next?

Accepting Help

Being open to accepting help from others during times of change.

If you're going through a change that's hard, like moving to a new place, it's okay to ask for help or a hug.

Friends and family are there to support you!

Who can you ask for help or support when dealing with a change?

The Puzzle of Life

Seeing how different pieces and changes fit together to make the whole.

Life is like a big puzzle, and each change is a new piece.

Sometimes it's hard to see where the piece fits, but eventually, it helps complete the beautiful picture of your life!

What change in your life is like a puzzle piece that will make sense later?

Accepting What We Cannot Change

Focusing energy on what we can control and accepting what we cannot.

You can't stop the rain, but you can choose to splash in the puddles!

Focus on what you can do, and let go of what you can't change.

This helps you feel happier and more in control.

What can you let go of today that you cannot change?

Growing Through Challenges

Challenges and changes help us grow stronger.

Just like muscles get stronger when you exercise, facing changes and challenges helps you grow stronger inside.

Embrace them as chances to become even more amazing!

What challenge have you faced recently that has caused you to grow?

The Adventure of Life

Life is an ever-changing journey full of surprises.

Imagine your life as an exciting adventure story, filled with unexpected twists and turns, just like your favorite books and movies.

Each day brings new surprises and challenges to explore.

Embrace these surprises, learn from them, and enjoy the journey every step of the way!

What recent surprise has become part of your adventure?

Chapter 8

Gratitude and Appreciation

Find happiness by being thankful for the people, experiences, and things that make your life special.

A Thankful Heart

Marcus Aurelius emphasizes appreciating the privilege of being alive and experiencing the world.

Every morning when you wake up, take a moment to be thankful for a new day.

Think about the sun shining, the birds singing, and the fun you might have.

A thankful heart makes your day brighter!

What are you thankful for this morning?

Appreciating Simple Joys

He encourages finding joy and gratitude in simple things.

You don't need big or fancy things to be happy.

Enjoying an ice cream cone, playing with a pet, or laughing with friends are special moments to appreciate.

These simple joys make life wonderful!

What simple joy can you appreciate today?

Gratitude Journal

Reflecting on what you're grateful for enhances appreciation.

Each day, think of three things you're thankful for.

Maybe it's your family, your favorite book, or a funny joke you heard.

Writing them down helps you remember how lucky you are!

What three things are you thankful for today?

Cherishing Friendships

Valuing the people in your life and the connections you share.

Friends are like treasures.

Be grateful for the laughs you share, the games you play, and the times they cheer you up.

Let them know how much they mean to you!

What can you do today to show a friend how much they mean to you?

Thanking Nature

Appreciating the natural world around us.

Take a moment to appreciate the trees that give us shade, the flowers that bring color, and the clouds that make fun shapes.

Nature is full of gifts for us to enjoy!

What part of nature can you thank and appreciate today?

The Gift of Learning

Being grateful for opportunities to learn and grow.

Every day is a chance to learn something new.

Be thankful for your teachers, books, and experiences that help you grow smarter and wiser!

What new thing have you learned today that you're grateful for?

Gratitude in Challenges

Finding things to appreciate even during difficult times.

Even when things are tough, like a hard test or a rainy day, try to find something good.

Maybe you learned something new or got to splash in puddles.

Finding the silver lining helps you stay positive!

What is something that is tough that you can still be grateful for?

Sharing Appreciation

Expressing gratitude to others encourages them and strengthens bonds.

Tell your family and friends why you appreciate them.

Maybe your sister makes you laugh, or your dad reads you stories.

Sharing your gratitude makes them feel loved and special!

Who can you share your appreciation with today?

Grateful for Yourself

Appreciating your own abilities and qualities.

Be thankful for who you are!

Maybe you're a good friend, a creative artist, or a fast runner.

Recognizing your own talents and qualities helps you feel happy and confident.

What is something about yourself that you're thankful for?

The Magic of Giving

Understanding that giving to others can bring joy and gratitude.

When you share or give to others, you spread happiness.

Seeing someone smile because of your kindness makes you feel grateful and joyful too!

What can you give or share today to spread happiness?

Thankful for Differences

Appreciating the diversity in people and experiences.

Everyone is different, and that's amazing!

Be grateful for the variety of cultures, ideas, and talents that make the world interesting and fun.

What difference in someone else can you appreciate today?

Gratitude for Challenges

Understanding that challenges help us grow, and being thankful for them.

When you face a challenge, like learning to tie your shoes or solving a tough puzzle, be grateful.

Overcoming it makes you stronger and teaches you new skills!

What challenge can you be thankful for because it helps you grow stronger?

Appreciating Effort

Recognizing and valuing the efforts others make for us.

Notice when someone puts effort into helping you, like your coach teaching you a new move or your friend helping you with a project.

Saying "Thanks for your help!" shows you appreciate their time and care.

If they feel appreciated, they are more likely to help you even more!

Whose effort can you appreciate and thank today?

Thanking Your Body

Being grateful for your health and what your body can do.

Your body does amazing things every day!

Be thankful for your legs that let you run, your eyes that let you see, and your heart that beats strong.

Taking care of your body shows appreciation for all it does.

What amazing thing can you thank your body for today?

The Gift of Imagination

Appreciating the ability to dream and imagine.

Your imagination is a wonderful gift!

Be grateful for the stories you create, the games you invent, and the dreams you have.

Your imagination makes life magical!

What will you use your imagination to create or dream about today?

Gratitude for Rest

Recognizing the importance of rest and relaxation.

Be thankful for cozy beds, bedtime stories, and the chance to rest.

Sleep helps you recharge so you can have energy for more fun tomorrow!

When you go to bed today, think about how great it is to be relaxed and resting.

Appreciating Kindness

Being grateful when others show kindness to you.

When someone is kind to you, like sharing their toys or giving you a hug when you're sad, let them know you appreciate it.

Kindness is a gift to be cherished!

Has someone been kind to you recently? Did you let them know you appreciate it? It's not too late.

Gratitude Every Day

Making gratitude a daily practice enriches life.

Try to find something to be grateful for each day.

It could be big or small.

Making gratitude a habit fills your life with happiness and love!

What can you be grateful for today to fill your heart with happiness?

CHAPTER 9

Patience and Perseverance

LEARN HOW BEING PATIENT AND NEVER GIVING UP HELPS YOU OVERCOME CHALLENGES AND REACH YOUR GOALS.

The Slow and Steady Turtle

Marcus Aurelius emphasizes the importance of patience and steady effort in achieving goals.

Remember the story of the turtle and the hare?

The turtle moved slowly but kept going and won the race!

When you work patiently and don't give up, you can achieve great things, just like the turtle.

What can you do today to be slow and steady like the turtle?

The Growing Seed

Understanding that some things take time to develop, and patience is essential.

When you plant a seed, it doesn't become a flower overnight.

It needs water, sunshine, and time to grow.

Patience helps you wait and enjoy watching it bloom!

What are you patiently waiting for that will take time to grow?

Practice Makes Perfect

Perseverance in practice leads to mastery.

Learning to play an instrument or a sport takes practice.

Even if it's hard at first, keep trying!

With patience and perseverance, you'll get better and better.

What skill are you practicing that will get better with time?

Overcoming Obstacles

Challenges are opportunities to strengthen perseverance.

If you come across a tricky math problem or a difficult puzzle, don't give up!

Take a deep breath, try again, and keep going.

Overcoming obstacles makes you stronger.

What challenge can you keep working on to grow stronger?

The Art of Patience

Patience is a virtue that brings peace of mind.

Being patient is like having a superpower that keeps you calm and happy.

When you wait patiently, you feel more relaxed and enjoy things more.

What can you practice being patient with today to feel more peaceful?

Small Steps Forward

Progress often comes in small, consistent steps.

Climbing a mountain starts with one step at a time.

Each small step brings you closer to the top.

Keep moving forward, and you'll reach your goals!

What small step can you take today to move closer to your goal?

Handling Frustration

Managing frustration is part of developing patience.

It's okay to feel frustrated when something is tough.

Take a moment to breathe, maybe count to ten, and then try again.

Handling frustration helps you stay patient and focused.

What's something you could do if you encounter a frustrating situation?

The Waiting Game

Learning to enjoy moments of waiting can cultivate patience.

Turn waiting into a game!

See how long you can stand on one foot or count how many different colors you can spot.

Making waiting fun helps time go by faster!

What game can you play while waiting to make it fun?

Patience with Others

Being patient with people helps build strong relationships.

If a friend is taking a long time to learn a game or tell a story, be patient and listen.

Your patience shows you care and makes your friendship stronger.

How can you be patient with someone today to show you care?

Never Giving Up

Perseverance is about continuing to try, even after failures.

If you fall off your bike while learning to ride, get back up and try again.

Each attempt brings you closer to success.

Never giving up is the key!

What is something you will keep trying, even if it's hard?

The Puzzle Piece

Patience is needed to see how all pieces fit together over time.

When working on a big puzzle, it might take time to find where each piece goes.

Patiently trying different spots helps you complete the picture.

What puzzle in life are you working on patiently right now?

The Calm Mind

A patient mind remains calm and clear, aiding in problem-solving.

When you're patient, your mind is like a still pond, clear and peaceful.

This helps you think better and solve problems more easily.

What can you do today to keep your mind calm and clear?

The Value of Persistence

Persistence leads to achieving goals that seemed difficult at first.

Remember when you couldn't tie your shoes, but you kept trying?

Now you can do it all by yourself!

Persistence helps you learn and grow.

What is something you can achieve if you keep trying?

Patience with Yourself

Being patient with oneself is important for personal development.

If you're learning something new and it's taking time, be kind and patient with yourself.

Everyone learns at their own pace, and that's okay!

What can you be patient with yourself about as you learn and grow?

The Storybook Journey

Enjoying the journey, not just the destination, teaches patience.

When reading a story, enjoy each chapter instead of rushing to the end.

The adventure along the way is what makes it exciting!

What can you enjoy today about your journey, rather than rushing to the end?

Waiting Your Turn

Patience is shown by waiting respectfully for your turn.

In games or conversations, waiting your turn shows respect and patience.

It makes playing and talking more fun for everyone!

How will you show patience by waiting your turn today?

The Mountain Stream

Slow and steady effort carves the path over time.

Just like water slowly shapes rocks over time, your steady efforts make a big difference.

Keep going, and you'll create something amazing!

What steady effort can you make today to create something wonderful in the future?

Celebrating Small Victories

Recognizing and appreciating progress encourages perseverance.

When you make progress, like reading a new word or learning a dance move, celebrate!

Each small victory is a step forward and deserves a happy dance!

What small victory can you celebrate today?

Afterword

Thank you for joining us on this journey through *The Kind Emperor*. Marcus Aurelius' wisdom has touched many lives for almost two thousand years, and it's my hope that these simple lessons have helped spark your own thoughts about kindness, courage, and living well.

Remember, these ideas aren't just for reading; they're meant to be practiced every day. Some days, you might find it easy to be patient or brave, and other days it may feel a bit harder. That's perfectly okay! What matters is the effort you make to keep growing, learning, and understanding yourself and others.

The journey to becoming kind, wise, and resilient is a lifelong one. Each small step you take, each moment you reflect, and every act of kindness adds to the strength of your character. I encourage you to keep exploring these ideas, finding what resonates with you, and making them your own.

Thank you again for reading, and may the wisdom of *The Kind Emperor* continue to be a guiding light as you grow.

Warm wishes,
B.J. Banks

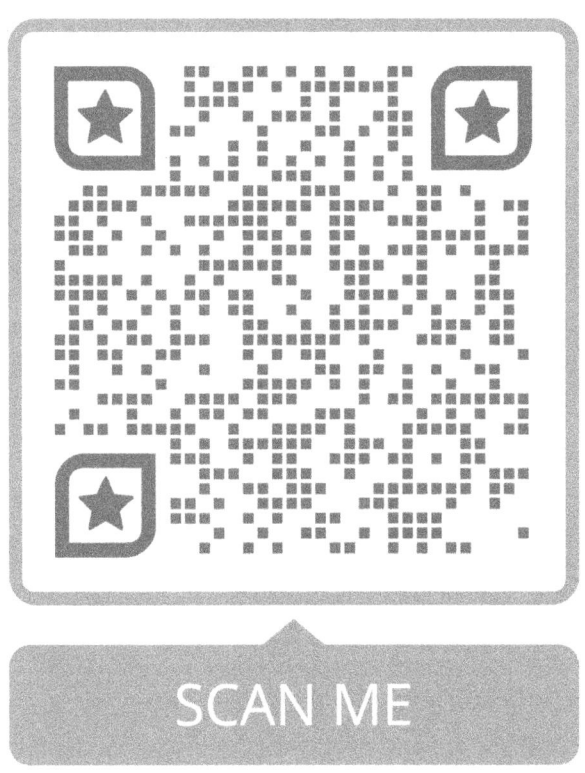

Free Gifts

As a thank you for purchasing The Kind Emperor, I have created 3 practical games and activities to further promote a stoic mindset at home.

www.ingramcontent.com/pod-product-compliance
Lightning Source LLC
Chambersburg PA
CBHW052140070526
44585CB00017B/1901